The Baby Cake: A Full Life Choice

Not

"Pro-Life" vs. "Pro-Choice"

By

Marjorie J. Frazier

1ˢᵗ Edition

The Baby Cake: A Full Life Choice

Not "Pro-Life" vs. "Pro-Choice"

Written by Marjorie J Frazier

Self-Published by Marjorie J Frazier

June 9, 2019

Written and Revised Dates:

2/12/17, Rev. 4/12/19,5/21, 5/22, 5/23, 5/29,
6/2, 6/6, 6/8, 6/9, 8/26

(This is a quick write up on the subject due to the current laws being implemented, but I welcome partners to assist in more research and providing a more extensive version of this topic.)

Preface

On the subject of Pro-Choice vs. Pro-Life...

It sounds like ONE EXTREME or THE OTHER, and honestly, I wonder how a person can completely agree with either? I truly think that these two opposing groups should try to work together rather than be at odds with one another.

Let's be honest: NO ONE WITH A HEART WANTS TO SEE A CHILD'S LIFE TERMINATED.

Furthermore, there are numerous situations that may cause a person to lean from one side to the other, but the honest truth is that neither is a solution to the problem. BOTH focus on making a decision during a brief period of time AFTER CONCEPTION.

However, there's more to bringing life into the world than that - certainly a lot more when it comes to establishing the foundations of and maintaining the blueprint of a viable human life.

Think of it as 'The Baby Cake'...

[Although it may seem a bit crude at first glance, this analogy stems from the old English phrase "bun in the oven" (Grammarist, n.d.)[1]]

---

[1] https://grammarist.com/idiom/bun-in-the-oven/

To have a *bun in the oven* means to be pregnant, to be expecting a child. The term *bun in the oven* has been traced to a novel published in 1951, *Cruel Sea* by Nicholas Monsarrat. Interestingly, a woman's womb has been referred to as an oven since the late 1600s, though it took nearly three hundred years for the imagery of a bun baking in that oven to become established. The plural form to mean a pregnancy in which more than one child is being carried would be *buns in the oven*. The plural form to mean multiple pregnant women would be *buns in the ovens*.

The Baby Cake: A Full Life Choice

Index

Chapter 1

Create Recipe

(Baby's Origin)

Babies don't ask to be born and have no control of the how, why and when.

As far as the HOW, we know that 'naturally' there are only two people who are fundamentally and critically responsible for the creation of a baby. Even so, in the case of an unplanned or unwanted pregnancy, it is typically the female who makes the final decision.

Regarding the WHY. Of course, there are many scenarios as to why a woman may find herself 'distressed and pregnant' (which is the main situation focused on in this book): teenage naïveté, prostitution, depression, drug addiction, sex addiction, rape, incest, etc.

Which brings us to the WHEN. There has been great debate as to the true beginning of life, whether it's a fertilized egg, the moment the heart beats, or once it becomes independent of the womb.[2] (Health N. I., n.d.)

---

[2] US National Library of Medicine, National Institute of Health, https://www.ncbi.nlm.nih.gov/pubmed/8303918
What is the legal definition of when life begins? The embryo protection **law** in force as of January 1, 1991, defines the beginning of **life** in a medical sense, to wit, the embryo is the fertilized egg cell capable of development already from the time of fertilization. ... No other **law** explicitly provides a similar **definition** of the appearance of early human **life**.

Many have wrestled with this subject, even former President Ronald Reagan, who is staunchly remembered as a 'champion of pro-life'.

"On June 14, 1967, Ronald Reagan signed the Therapeutic Abortion Act, after only six months as California governor… he decided to do what he could to make the bill less harmful, arguing for the insertion of certain language that eliminated its worst features and allowed for abortion only in rare cases — such as rape or incest, or where pregnancy would gravely impair the physical or mental health of the mother." (Doerner, 2008)

However, as president (1981 – 1989), he made a complete about-face as written in his 1983 book, Abortion and the Conscience of the Nation. "I have often said that when we talk about abortion, we are talking about two lives—the life of the mother and the life of the unborn child. Why else do we call a pregnant woman a mother? I have also said that anyone who doesn't feel sure whether we are talking about a second human life should clearly give life the benefit of the doubt. If you don't know whether a body is alive or dead, you would never bury it. I think this consideration itself should be enough for all of us to insist on protecting the unborn." (Anderson, 2013)

So this is not to disparage President Reagan's decision to change his mind once he devoted more attention to the issue. It's simply to say that anyone may compelled to change their mind on a subject they once had a long-standing position on, when they pursue more information and perhaps try to look at things from an objective lens.

When we understand that we are not locked in to anyone else's preconceived notions, able to freely generate our own thoughts and ideas, then I think that we'll be able to find a universal and humanitarian solution for all concerned on this issue.

In her 2019 Commencement Speech at American University, Washington D.C., Stacey Abrams (2018 Georgia Gubernatorial Candidate and founder of Fair Fight Action) said it well, "...being 'pro this' or 'anti-that' becomes an excuse for lazy thinking. And for today, at least, I urge you to set aside your labels and explore what your principals say about the world you wish to serve." (Abrams, 2019)

CHAPTER 2

"Preheat the Oven"

(Hormones & Sexual Curiosity)

The conversation about sex should start at home, but probably doesn't for most people. It remains one of the most uncomfortable subjects that is discussed between a parent and a child, but even young children want to know where baby's come from. And the questions get more specific with each growing age.

As pre-teens and teenagers, their bodies begin to go through the natural physical hormonal development, and their sexuality becomes more prevalent.

In any event, as parents, guardians and caretakers we need to be more prepared. There are many books, videos, etc. that can aide us. If schools are offering sexual education training, maybe you should allow your child to participate. If there are seminars for them or for families, you could attend them together. This is science, biology. We need to learn the intricacies of sexuality and parenthood at the appropriate time, just as we study basic subjects – and just as we SHOULD study finance and money management.

Otherwise, your children will learn from their peers, from their non-peers or even by accident!

In addition, we must instill in our boys that THEY WILL BE RESPONSIBLE if they impregnate a girl. Also, that they will and should share in every action and decision that is made regarding their joint creation. Furthermore, our laws must address and enforce this issue starting at the pre-birth stage to ensure that this child is supported to the maximum level.

Creating laws to cover the entire phase of a child's life is not so far-fetched. We already have 200-year- old laws on the books about sexual activity (fornication, adultery, etc.), and as antiquated as they may be, perhaps they can be modified and expanded to PROTECT THE FULL LIFE OF A CHILD. (Law, n.d.) (Grossman, 2005) (Greenwood, 2013)

CHAPTER 3

"Gather the Ingredients"

(Romantic Thoughts & Endeavors)

When pheromones jump into over-drive, the game is on! Attraction can be based on physical appearance, attitude, intellect, talent, etc. Young love can happen immediately or in a short span, but very seldom over a long period of time. Falling in love (or just 'in-like' for some) will supersede logic most times, and usually happens unexpectedly.

Obviously, this is a very critical time in an adolescent's life. If they don't have the right emotional support or mental tools, it can be devastating.

For girls who grew up without father's in the household, many times, they don't have a foundation on how to approach boys, or how to allow themselves to be approached. There is also that inner craving to have some type of man in their lives.

By the same token, adolescent boys who didn't have a father or father-figure in their lives are typically ill-prepared to deal with their own sexuality and relationships.

Then there is also the issue of rape, incest, etc. In these situations, a new rule of law that emphasizes the responsibility of the father (perhaps financially rather than emotionally) would be extremely helpful.

We must find better ways to identify and resolve these issues. If not, they will continue to become a vicious generational cycle.

CHAPTER 4

"Mise en Place" or Assemble Ingredients & Equipment

(Birth Control Methods)

Preparation or No Preparation? The thoughts are constantly in their minds, part of their daily conversations with their friends, in the music they listen to, the movies they view... and yes – even in their dreams.

Do they have proficient knowledge about birth control and contraceptives? Abstention, of course, is the truest form of birth control, but if your child is tempted or prone to sexual activity, they should receive the proper support and guidance, and any specialized advice from a licensed medical professional or practitioner.

The most effective parenting that I've discovered, as far as parents actually discussing the subject earlier rather than later, resulted in most of the children avoiding the 'pregnancy setback' and going on to be high achievers in their field and/or happily married.

If parents can get over the hump and pierce through the uncomfortableness of discussing sex with their very insightful and eager children, I believe that more will be able to navigate these murky waters through their adolescence and into adulthood. Also, there is more education material (i.e. books, video, digital info, etc.) available than ever before.

CHAPTER 5

"Mix It Up"

(Sexual Experience)

The moment has come, for better or worse. Are they strong enough to say 'No'?

If not, do they know how to use preventative devices or are they swimming without a paddle?

Like anything else in life, it's better to come prepared than to wing it – which obviously leads to more accidents. (Of course, if this was a forced act, then it's a moot point.)

A few things to consider is how was the environment created that allowed for this action? Where were the parents? What was the parent-youth relationship? Were there signs that the youth was acting differently, distancing themselves, acting out, socializing with atypical friends, etc.? - These flags are something that parents should be on the alert for in general (i.e. drug experimentation, suicidal thoughts, etc.).

One more thing: Just because someone is a card-carrying birth control taker who is actively practicing sex, although avoiding pregnancy, doesn't give them any more right to judgment over a woman that has found herself pregnant and visible for the world to see. Each would be in violation of any perceived moral or legal law, as are still complicit in 'the act'.

Bottom Line: Once someone crosses the threshold from virginity into sexual activity, they are exposed to a Pandora's box of possibilities (as well as being susceptible to various sexually transmitted diseases that could have long lasting effects). Ideally, this should be planned, or at the utmost taken just as seriously as making their most valuable purchase or biggest life's decision. For many, however, it will be unplanned. Still, all support systems available should help the individual understand the gravity of it all.

CHAPTER 6

"Throw It in the Oven"

(Conception)

What just happened? Is this real? - Where did he go???

While teen pregnancy had appeared to decrease about 7% from 2016 to 2017, there was still nearly 200,000 babies born to females 15 to 19 years of age (amounting to about 19 out of every 1000 females giving birth). Evidence suggests that some reasons for the decline may be due to more teens abstaining or the use of more birth control methods. (Reproductive Health: Teen Pregnancy, n.d.)

Not too surprising is the fact that Hispanic and Black teen birth rates were twice as high as that of their White counterparts. Even more alarming is that American Indian and Alaska Native teens had the highest birth rate among all races and ethnicities. (Reproductive Health: Teen Pregnancy, n.d.)

Furthermore, the report states:

"Less favorable socioeconomic conditions, such as low education and low income levels of a teen's family, may contribute to high teen birth rates. Teens in child welfare systems are at higher risk of teen pregnancy and birth than other groups. For example, young women living in foster care are more than twice as likely to become pregnant than those not in foster care." (Reproductive Health: Teen Pregnancy, n.d.)

This clearly demonstrates that a higher amount of energy and resources needs to be directed towards: Hispanic, Black, American Indian and Native Alaskan teens. And we must not forget that the youth who are less educated, in lower income brackets or in foster care are crying out for help!

Of course, a 'distressed pregnancy' can happen to both the young and old, putting them in a position to make a life-altering choice.

Just read the scenarios below and think about how many people you know that fall into some of these categories:

#1: Teenage Naïveté: A teenage girl gets pregnant after having her first sexual relations with a teenage boy. Since the boy naturally denies being the father, the girl and her family are left with the responsibility of whether to continue the pregnancy and step into motherhood, or have her focus on completing her education.

#2: Discarded: A wayward and unwanted girl living in a foster home has never had familial support and seeks sexual relations so that she can have a child of her own to finally feel loved.

#3: Seduced by Power: A clergy illicitly fathers a child with one of his female members. Even though he espouses "pro-life" publicly, privately he has supported and paid for the abortion of his lover.

#4: Career Driven: A single career woman unexpectedly finds herself pregnant after having an affair with a co-worker. She is trying to work her way up the corporate ladder and feels that having a child, particularly out-of-wedlock, will thwart her chances of rising successfully.

#5: Rape: A young girl is kidnapped, traumatized and repeatedly RAPED by her captor, which results in her giving birth to a child.

#6: Incest: A girl is molested by an alcoholic father, then is further emotionally tormented when she discovers she's pregnant.

#7: Life in Jeopardy: A sickly expected mother doesn't have the physical strength to bring her fetus to full term without sacrificing her own life.

While there are numerous roads that lead to conception, there are few choices to be made afterwards:

1) Deliver

2) Terminate or

3) Give the child away

Along with that decision comes the weight of economics, religion, politics, government, society, etc.

Some of the cultural and societal impacts may be as follows:

#1: Extremist: A wealthy, card-carrying "Pro-Lifer", devout Christian who's against abortion at any cost spends most of his money for TRAVEL, HOMES, CLOTHING, JEWELRY, etc. while none is used for donating and supporting the aged-out foster girl who can't get affordable housing for herself and her young family.

#2: Birth Control User: A privileged female, who has used assisted birth control methods to stifle the outcome of her sexual encounters, prefers to criticize rather than SUPPORT the impoverished couple down the street who are struggling to raise 6 kids.

#3: Confused & Trapped: A female who is at crossroads about her decision to give birth, believes in the sanctity of life but is conflicted about when the moment of life begins.

#4: Illegal Abortion: A man is driving his pregnant girlfriend to an unlicensed practitioner to perform an emergency abortion on her, that results in serious complications.

#5: Falsely Labeled Due to Planned Parenthood Association: A 'pro-life leaning' rural woman visits the closest Planned Parenthood facility for an affordable cancer screening, but is recognized by a neighbor upon leaving and is gossiped about and frowned upon by her local community.

CHAPTER 7

"Check on the Baking"

(Decision Time)

Now is the time to get down to the 'nitty gritty'. Many things can happen during the pregnancy. Prematurity, transfer of drugs, severe deformity or inability to maintain a viable life, etc.

However, barring miscarriage or other accidental loss of the child, the time for a life or death decision has to be made.

On one hand, it seems to be a fine and noble stance to claim that one is Pro-Life, against ending the life of an innocent child. – But is that enough? End of story?

One the other hand, it appears that a more private and progressive decision is to be Pro-Choice, supporting the independent right of mother to make her own personal decision to carry the baby or not. According to Justice Ruth Bader Ginsburg,

> *"The decision whether or not to bear a child is central to a woman's life, to her well-being and dignity. It is a decision she must make for herself. When Government controls that decision for her, she is being treated as less than a fully adult human responsible for her own choices."* (Ginsburg, 2019)

Could it be as simple as that? I partially agree. Yes, it is the woman's body, health and physical journey but she did not conceive the child alone and it isn't only her blood and DNA that courses through it. If this school of thought is supported, and it is to be a "personal" choice, then it should first be attempted to be a joint decision between the parents.

Of course, if one considers the 'broader picture' which I have expanded upon in this book, I believe that many will rethink the premise of the initial debate (Pro-Choice vs. Pro-Life).

CHAPTER 8

"Cool Down"

(The Baby Is Born – Now What?)

We need to stop this nonsense of having the unwed girl (and her family) solely responsible for taking care of newborn, without any forced responsibility on the father (and his family, if a minor).

Laws should be created to make it mandatory that the biological father is jointly responsible from the day of conception for medical and financial expenses. In fact, it should be mandatory that BOTH young parents go to the doctor appointments and hospital delivery together. They both created the baby, and they both should share in the responsibility from the beginning. If the boy doesn't voluntarily participate, then once the child is born, an immediate DNA test should be taken to confirm his paternity, and then he should be fined for missing those appointments, as well as for their share of any expenses. Not only is this the fair thing to do, but it is also a deterrent to themselves and their peers from repeating the same mistake.

MOST IMPORTANTLY, it's about PUTTING THE BABY FIRST. The child did not ask to be born, and now that it's here – BOTH PARENTS are responsible to give it the very best they have for the remainder of the it's lifetime.

CHAPTER 9

"Frost the Cake"

(Feeding, Clothing, Sheltering)

Both parents (and families) should be involved in making concrete plans and share in the present and future life of the child.

The immediate need is for food, clothing, shelter and medical.

All divisiveness and animosity must be dissolved as a united front should be formed between families for the well-being of the child. If this can't happen automatically, then that's when our judicial system should step in to ensure that the child is protected.

CHAPTER 10

"May I Have a Slice?"

(Slices of a Lifetime)

Psalm 82:3 (KJV Bible)

"Defend the poor and the fatherless;

Do justice to the poor and the needy."

What will the outcome be? How will society treat this child through the stages of his/her life? (The Child Development Institute, n.d.)

Will it set them up for disaster or guide them to success? Will they be destined to serving a lifetime of disenfranchisement or one of franchise?

Is every child of equal value as the next? Is someone who is born with a wooden spoon on par with someone born with a silver one? Who can predict the destiny of a soul on earth, whether one will become a non-productive citizen or a life-saving surgeon?

In 1983, President Reagan posed the question, "The real question is not when life begins, but: 'What is the value of a human life?'"… Current research indicates that the average life time of an American citizen is about 79 years (Health V. W., n.d.) and the monetary value of a human life was estimated to be about $7.6 million as of 2010. Unfortunately, per the author, J. Mario Molina, Sen. Mitch McConnell directed the drafting of the "Better Care Act" that resulted in the value of an American life being reduced to about $1.2 million. (Molina, 2017)

I would lean towards the $7.6 million value, although I feel that it's difficult to attach a price to any life.

Regardless of any value assigned, the Declaration of Independence (July 4, 1776) states, "...all men are created equal... endowed by their Creator with... Life, Liberty and the pursuit of Happiness." (Life Liberty and the Pursuit of Happiness, n.d.)

Chapter 11

Standardize the Recipe

("Create Responsible and Sensible Laws")

We have been back-and-forth on the laws regarding the reproductive rights of women. From the Texas Statute of 1961 which criminalized abortion unless a women's life was at risk (Texas Abortion Statutes, n.d.), to the 1973 Supreme Court Decision of Roe vs. Wade which legalized abortion (Roe v Wade: Its History and Impact, n.d.), to today's fast-sprouting litigation beginning in key states such as Alabama and Missouri that aim to re-criminalize women (and doctors) who abort between the 6th to 8th week of fetal development. (Details of Abortion Legislation, n.d.)

Unfortunately, time and time again, we find that many of the people in power, that espouse the strictest rules and laws, are the ones that are committing the most heinous violations.

I defy these knee-jerk and biased directives, when we have too many instances of influential people abusing the system for their own devices, hidden under the cloud of religious authority, unabashed fame or political power.

Instead of pushing lopsided laws that are geared towards penalizing the mothers and doctors, there should be stronger laws created to ensure that the mother and father are jointly responsible (in every way) for the child's livelihood.

If the parents (and their families) can't handle it with their own resources, then the government (and our 'concerned' society) should step in to make sure that these babies have the basic needs: housing, medical, food, clothing, education, etc. until they become independent adults themselves.

Finally, we must get at the root and cause. Every citizen must be treated with respect and value. We need to choose representatives that will fight aggressively to equalize education, jobs, health and wealth opportunities; will work to prevent whole communities from being immersed into poverty, unemployment, addiction, incarceration, mental disorders, etc. and help to avoid creating the next generation of the 'distressed and pregnant'.

The Baby Cake Approach (Full Life Choice) may not be an absolute REPLACEMENT for either the Pro-Life or Pro-Choice Argument, but it certainly can help steer us in a more comprehensive and wholesome approach to solving the issue of a distressed and unplanned birth.

We can do it. We can all do it if we rise to the moral and humanitarian standards that our country was built on.

Bibliography

Abrams, S. (2019, May 11). *American University Commencement Address*. Retrieved from C-
    Span: https://www.c-span.org/video/?460668-1/stacey-abrams-commencement-speech-
    american-university

Anderson, R. T. (2013). *Reagan's Legacy: The Sacred Value of Human Life*. Retrieved from
    Daily Signal: https://www.dailysignal.com/2013/02/07/reagans-legacy-the-sacred-value-
    of-human-life/

Details of Abortion Legislation. (n.d.). Retrieved from http://time.com/5591166/state-abortion-
    laws-explained/: http://time.com/5591166/state-abortion-laws-explained/

Doerner, P. K. (2008). *Reagans Darkest Hour*. Retrieved from National Review:
    https://www.nationalreview.com/2008/01/reagans-darkest-hour-paul-kengor-patricia-
    clark-doerner/

Ginsburg, J. R. (2019, June 3rd). Roe vs Wade Update by DSCC.

Grammarist. (n.d.). *Bun In The Oven*. Retrieved from Grammarist.com:
    https://grammarist.com/idiom/bun-in-the-oven/

Greenwood, A. (2013). *Wierd Laws*. Retrieved from Huffington Post:
    https://www.huffpost.com/entry/virginia-weird-laws_n_4260541

Grossman, J. (2005). *Old Laws*. Retrieved from CNN.com:
    http://www.cnn.com/2005/LAW/01/25/grossman.oldlaws/

Health, N. I. (n.d.). *US National LIbrary of Medicine*. Retrieved from National Institute of
    Health: https://www.ncbi.nlm.nih.gov/pubmed/8303918

Health, V. W. (n.d.). *Human Life Span*. Retrieved from Very Well Health:

    https://www.verywellhealth.com/what-is-the-human-life-span-2223929

Law, V. (n.d.). *Fornication*. Retrieved from Law.Lis.Virginia.Gov:

    https://law.lis.virginia.gov/vacode/title18.2/chapter8/section18.2-344/

Life Liberty and the Pursuit of Happiness. (n.d.). Retrieved from Wikipedia:

    https://en.wikipedia.org/wiki/Life,_Liberty_and_the_pursuit_of_Happiness

Molina, J. M. (2017). *The Value of Human Life*. Retrieved from Morning Consult:

    https://morningconsult.com/opinions/value-human-life

Reproductive Health: Teen Pregnancy. (n.d.). Retrieved from Centers for Disease Control:

    https://www.cdc.gov/teenpregnancy/about/index.htm

Reproductive Health: Teen Pregnancy. (n.d.). Retrieved from Centers for Disease Control:

    https://www.cdc.gov/nchs/products/databriefs/db318.htm

Reproductive Health: Teen Pregnancy. (n.d.). Retrieved from Centers for Disease Control:

    https://www.cdc.gov/teenpregnancy/about/index.htm

Roe v Wade: Its History and Impact. (n.d.). Retrieved from Planned Parenthood:

    https://www.plannedparenthoodaction.org/uploads/filer_public/c6/59/c65961ce-447c-

    48e1-b315-79bfac151e42/abortion_roe_history.pdf

Texas Abortion Statutes. (n.d.). Retrieved from Wikipedia:

    https://en.wikipedia.org/wiki/Texas_abortion_statutes_(1961)

The Child Development Institute. (n.d.). *The Ages and Stages of Child Development*. Retrieved

    from The Child Development Institute: https://childdevelopmentinfo.com/ages-

    stages/#.XLBYoOhKiM8

www.ingramcontent.com/pod-product-compliance
Lightning Source LLC
Chambersburg PA
CBHW021000180526
45163CB00006B/2437